To Help You Recall ...

MINI &
MEMORIES

For Image Bearers

JOANNE WALLACE

*To everyone who needs daily
"heart hugs" and the reminder
that we are God's image bearer.*

*May this book encourage you to
become more conformed to His
image.*

*"...Being confident of this, that He
who began a good work in you
will carry it on to completion..."
(Phil. 1:6, NIV)*

*In His Image,
Joanne
Wallace*

ACKNOWLEDGEMENTS

To the women who have shared their lives and experiences so that I may continue to grow and learn to be more conformed to HIS image.

To my daughter, Deanna, whose editing and lay-out skills made this book possible.

I am grateful for the many people who have contributed comments or quotes for this book. Any slight in not giving credit where credit is due is unintentional. If anything is credited incorrectly I would be grateful if readers would contact me with the original source.

ISBN: 1-880527-03-0

MINI MEMORIES

For Image Bearers

By Joanne Wallace

Conference Office
P.O. Box 2213
Fremont, CA 94536

DEDICATION

*To my mother, Mary Gibson,
who even now at 86 years young,
has a twinkle in her eye and
laughter in her voice. Her love
and prayers are a great source
of inspiration as she continues
to bear God's image to me.*

CONTENTS

IMAGE BEARING

IMAGE BEARING

Love is a choice.

Love is not a feeling, but love creates feelings.

Love is a decision.

Love is action...something that you DO!

IMAGE BEARING

...abound in love, one toward another...

I Thess. 3:12 (KJV)

The three most important words to say today, "I love you."

IMAGE BEARING

Accepting others means loving unconditionally. It means differentiating between the value of a person and the mistakes they make.

Accept one another, then; just as Christ accepted you, in order to bring praise to God.

Rom. 15:7 (NIV)

IMAGE BEARING

Hugs are needed for daily survival!

Hugs are needed for daily growth!

Hugs are needed for daily maintenance!

Determine that today you will hug with your whole heart...let your arms express your heart.

IMAGE BEARING

Everyone needs love and acceptance.
No one is perfect.

Everyone makes mistakes.

Everyone has weaknesses, faults and
hang-ups.

Everyone needs love and acceptance.

IMAGE BEARING

Jesus hung out with a lot of "undesirable" people. He was the "friend of sinners." Jesus did not condone sin, but he accepted the people unconditionally.

It is the same for you and me. Our Lord will not always approve of everything we do, but He will always accept us because He loves us!

IMAGE BEARING

A positive attiude is a choice.

I must spend consistent, daily time with God. Sometimes He speaks softly and I might miss what He is saying if I am not in tune with Him every day.

In many instances, you may be the only world's Bible.

IMAGE BEARING

Do you feel distant from God?
Spend daily, consistent time
with Him.   To cultivate any
friendship you must have
regular communication.
God is waiting for you.
He won't come in uninvited.

Are you leaving God in the
"waiting room?"

IMAGE BEARING

*You are not responsible for
another person's response.*

*You are only responsible
for your response.*

IMAGE BEARING

Discouraged people don't need critics. They hurt enough already.

Hurting people need a place to hide and heal.

God alone is capable of judging behavior. Your job is to love your neighbor.

IMAGE BEARING

There are two things you must do if you want to be attractive to others:

1. *listen*

2. *keep secrets*

IMAGE BEARING

If you love someone...you will always believe in him, and always expect the best of him...

I Cor. 13:7 (TLB)

"I'll love you forever, I'll like you for always."

--Robert Munsch

IMAGE BEARING

Three facts of life:
Everyone has a hurt.
Everyone needs encouragement.
Everyone needs a lift.

Change usually requires patience.
"Inch by inch is a cinch,
yard by yard is hard!"

IMAGE BEARING

Do you want to know how to change your mate?

Do you want to know how to change your child?

Treat them the way you want them to BECOME!

IMAGE BEARING

*One of life's greatest gifts
is to give encouragement
to everyone you meet.*

Edify means "to build up."

*Let us then pursue
what makes for peace
and for mutual upbuilding.*

Rom. 14:19 (RSV)

IMAGE BEARING

When many people in the world are tearing each other down, believers ought to be building each other up.

Walk the talk--or don't talk it!

IMAGE BEARING

God loves me. I am His child.
He celebrates each new step
I take in learning to be conformed
to His image.

Please be patient with me.
I'm still under construction.
God is not through with me yet!

God does not make junk!

IMAGE BEARING

*Being confident of this,
that He who began a good work
in you will carry it on to
completion until the day
of Christ Jesus.*

Phil. 1:6 (NIV)

*Let this mind be in you, which was
also in Jesus Christ.*

Phil. 2:5 (NKJV)

WHO AM I?

WHO AM I?

There is no contradiction between good mental health and Christian living. God made them to be fit together--to be knit in compatibility.

For in Him (God) we live, and move, and have our being...

Acts 17:28 (NKJV)

WHO AM I?

If we see ourselves as "rotten" though "forgiven" sinners, we will never measure up. This belief will lead to a sense of failure and a poor self-image. It is necessary to be "reprogrammed" to develop a healthier self-image.

...be transformed by the renewal of your mind...

Romans 12:2 (RSV)

WHO AM I?

*We were created in
God's image. His image
can be seen in our ability to:*
feel
think
choose
communicate
create
be self-aware
be morally-aware
be spiritually-aware

--Dr. Larry Day

WHO AM I?

*God's evaluation of you
is not dependent on the
currently popular body type,
but on His unchangeable
standard of unconditional love.*

*Your self-worth is a settled issue.
It was settled at the
cross of Calvary.*

WHO AM I?

If you hold on to God's truths about your value as a person, then you'll know who you are and be secure in yourself.

God's standard of unconditional love, forgiveness, and esteem toward you is the only standard on which you can depend. It doesn't change. He loves you just the way you are.

WHO AM I?

*SELF-IMAGE = how you see
yourself*

*SELF-ESTEEM = how you feel
about yourself*

*SELF-WORTH = how God sees
you*

WHO AM I?

For you created my inmost being; you knit me together in my mother's womb. I praise you because I am fearfully and wonderfully made; your works are wonderful, and I know that full well.

Psalm 139:13-14 (NIV)

...my inner self knows right well.

Psalm 139:14 (AMP)

...and that my soul knoweth right well.

Psalm 139:14 (KJV)

WHO AM I?

God's Word says your self-esteem is not based on whether you succeed or fail.

Your self-worth rests in the truth that God loves you totally and unconditionally. In God's eyes, through Christ, you are completely forgiven.

WHO AM I?

*We would worry less about
what other people think of us
if we realized how seldom
they do!*

--Ethel Barrett

"The me I see is the me I'll be."

(see Prov. 23:7)

*Self-esteem is like a deeply felt
self-picture we carry at the
center of our hearts.*

WHO AM I?

Verbal abuse crushes self-esteem.

A soothing tongue is a tree of life, but perversion in it crushes the spirit.

Prov. 15:4 (NAS)

"Words can sting like anything, but silence breaks the heart."

--Phyllis McGinley

WHO AM I?

Don't allow past experiences to cloud your future.

DECIDE to start over.

If you wait for perfect conditions you will never get anything done.

Ecc. 11:4 (TLB)

WHO AM I?

Turn off the television. It can be a waste of your time.

Begin today to read a good book or write a love letter to a friend.

WHO AM I?

You CAN get out of your rut.
Take action and begin today.
It is up to YOU.

Set realistic goals. Get out
your pen and paper. Write it
down. Formulate a plan.

I'd rather wear out than rust out!

WHO AM I?

Integrity and honesty have everything to do with a positive self-esteem.

Sinful practice has a powerful, negative influence on our self-esteem. With God's help, turn from that destruction.

WHO AM I?

Jesus said, "So watch out that the sunshine isn't blotted out. If you are filled with light within, with no dark corners, then your face will be radiant too, as though a floodlight is beamed upon you."

Luke 11:35-36 (TLB)

WHO AM I?

Hang in there! Don't give up!
Don't give up on
your optimism or your vision.
George Washington never
gave up.
Abraham Lincoln never
gave up.
Oliver Twiddledeedee...
Who's he?
See--you don't know him,
because he gave up!

--Lacy Able

WHO AM I?

*God got terribly excited when
you were born because He
saw the possibility of changing
the world through you.*

--Dr. Harold Ivan Smith

WHO AM I?

We are pressed on every side by troubles, but not crushed and broken. We are perplexed because we don't know why things happen as they do, but we don't give up and quit.

We get knocked down, but we get up again and keep going.

II Cor. 4:8 (TLB)

WHO AM I?

Never, ever quit!

Pray for a new dream!

Dream a new dream!

God loves me
just the way I am...
but too much to leave me
this way!

WHO AM I?

The blueprint for your life is written in your natural talents, abilities, and gifts.

Set as your top goal for this year to seek and find your special God-given gifts. Then use them!

I can do all things through Christ which strengtheneth me.

Phil. 4:13 (KJV)

WHO AM I?

*Each has his own special gift
from God, one of one kind and
one of another.*

I Cor. 7:7 (RSV)

*Your God-given gift, plus
diligence equals satisfaction.*

WHO AM I?

*Where there is no vision,
the people perish...*

Prov. 29:18 (KJV)

*You are the only person in the
world who can dream your
dream and have the strength
to make it come true!*

Never give up your dream!

WHO AM I?

Stop destructive comparison!
Comparison brings depression.

Let everyone be sure that he is
doing his very best, for then
he will have the personal
satisfaction of work well done,
and won't need to compare himself
with someone else.

Gal. 6:4 (TLB)

WHO AM I?

DAILY PRAYER:

Lord, I ask you to reprogram me with the truth that I am worthwhile and valuable, until it is deep within my innermost feelings.

WHO AM I?

*I am an image bearer of God!
This is a privilege and a
responsibility.*

*I am okay, justified, and
forgiven because of Jesus Christ.*

*My self-concept is not based on
performance.*

WHO AM I?

My self-concept is based on the truth of God's unconditional love and forgiveness.

Because of this truth, I am free to grow in personal ways and to demonstrate my own uniqueness.

LET'S COMMUNICATE!

LET'S COMMUNICATE!

...for a man's heart determines his speech.

Matt. 12:34 (TLB)

Whatever is in the heart overflows into speech.

Luke 6:45 (TLB)

Every word spoken comes from what fills the heart.

LET'S COMMUNICATE!

How you communicate builds or destroys someone's self-esteem. Negative talk is deadly.

Good communication occurs when an intended message is accurately received by another. This brings closeness in relationships and clarification in communicating.

Don't walk away from negative people--run!

LET'S COMMUNICATE!

*Anyone who finds the need to
say cutting or insulting remarks
about another person is
crying out with a
low self-esteem.*

*Attack the problem...
not the person*

*Good communication
always builds
a healthy self-esteem.*

LET'S COMMUNICATE!

*When you and I stop talking
to each other we're in
BIG trouble!*

*To open someone's heart to
communication, try these
simple phrases:
"Tell me more about it."
"What happened?"*

LET'S COMMUNICATE!

God has created you to have feelings. Feelings are not sinful or wrong. It is the ACTION that you take with your feelings that will determine the right or wrong.

If you stuff your feelings deep inside, they won't stay there. They will come out in either destructive or constructive ways.

LET'S COMMUNICATE!

*It is not so much what
you say as how you say it.*

*"Leveling" means sharing
how you feel,
but speaking the truth
in love.*

(See Eph. 4:15, 25)

LET'S COMMUNICATE!

*To effectively communicate
with someone, you must
validate their feelings,
whether you agree with them
or not.*

*Your arms were created
to wrap around someone!*

LET'S COMMUNICATE!

*There are three sentences
that need to be spoken
every day to the people
closest to you:*

*I love you.
I appreciate you.
I'm proud of you.*

LET'S COMMUNICATE!

Listening doesn't mean you have to "fix it."

Listen carefully to someone's problem and then simply ask, "Is there anything I can do to help?"

Listening does not require you to give advice...unless you are asked.

LET'S COMMUNICATE!

Don't "should" on others.

Don't talk so much...be sensible and turn off the flow.

Prov. 10:19 (TLB)

Relating is listening.

RELATIONSHIPS

RELATIONSHIPS

Intimacy...

*An intimate relationship is one
in which I feel safe.
It is revealing hopes, dreams,
fears and the past,
including sins and mistakes.
I can share these things
without the fear of being
judged, condemned,
or straightened out.*

--Author Unknown

RELATIONSHIPS

An intimate relationship means:

Holding a confidence--never passing on anything without the other person's consent.

Giving the other person "space"--never being a pest or acting possessive.

Sharing your inner self--not just listening to the other person, but being transparent yourself.

RELATIONSHIPS

Intimacy begins with you.

*YOU choose to nourish
a relationship.*

*Will you decide to invest your
time and yourself in an
intimate relationship?*

RELATIONSHIPS

Help me, Lord, to keep my mouth shut and my lips sealed.

Psalm 141:3 (TLB)

Truth must be married to love, honesty connected to kindness.

Revealing my feeling is the beginning of healing.

RELATIONSHIPS

A compliment is a word of love and you squelch this love when you don't accept it graciously.

Not accepting a compliment is insulting the giver of the compliment.

To accept a compliment, say "thank you." It's a simple, beautiful reply.

RELATIONSHIPS

It's not the things we do for ourselves that brings peace and contentment, but the things we do for other people.

Caring makes another person feel important.

We live up to the expectations others have of us.

FORGIVENESS

FORGIVENESS

The most beautiful thing you can do is to forgive.

Once God forgives, He never remembers nor reminds you of it again.

Keep short accounts with God.

FORGIVENESS

You have the option of moving and growing beyond your present situation.

Unexpressed anger comes out in your actions...and usually on innocent people.

Feelings of anger are normal when you lose something important to you.

FORGIVENESS

You can choose to make the most of your situation by working through your feelings and learning to trust again.

Risking and trusting may involve pain, but so does not risking and trusting.

FORGIVENESS

*Have continual "heart checks."
Do you need to ask for
forgiveness?*

*We often need "housecleaning
of the soul."*

*Daily confession:
"Lord, I blew it today. Please
make my heart right."*

FORGIVENESS

You cannot out sin God's grace.

Jesus stays with us in our failures. No matter how "big" our sin. With Christ, we can be forgiven and start over again.

The past ended one second ago!

FORGIVENESS

Life is like an onion,
you peel off one layer
at a time.

It's okay to take the time
to heal.

Sins are not "classified" with
the Lord.

FORGIVENESS

When someone has hurt you it may not be possible to forgive them immediately.

Sometimes it seems almost unnatural to forgive. A sense of fairness says that the other person should pay for what they have done. But, we must forgive.

Forgiveness doesn't make the other person right... it sets you free.

FORGIVENESS

God says, "My grace is sufficient for you." It is possible to forgive because of God's grace.

Forgiveness is not a feeling. It is a choice. A decision.

Always forgive your enemies... nothing annoys them so much.

--Oscar Wilde

FORGIVENESS

Forgiveness increases emotional health!

Forgiveness means letting go. You've cut the strings.

Sometimes we choose not to forgive because we want to get back at our offender, but we are the ones that are hurt by bitterness.

FORGIVENESS

Forgiveness is releasing your offender to God. You decide not to take revenge, but will let God do the work that needs to be done.

There are personal consequences to pay for our sins, but we can still be forgiven.

FORGIVENESS

*Forgiveness does not mean
that you continue to stay in
an abusive situation,
or that you allow the abuse
to go on without doing
something about it.*

*Crimes are serious and tragic
and leave devastation.
There are penalties to pay,
but there can still be
forgiveness.*

FORGIVENESS

Jesus is the "wounded healer."

Don't be afraid to seek help and counseling for life's wounds.

Friends can support you.
Counselors can guide you.
But only Jesus Christ
can heal you.

--Fred & Florence Littauer

FORGIVENESS

Forgiveness is felt when the bitterness and resentment is gone and you can wish the person well.

Forgiveness is a way of life--you never stop forgiving.

God can forgive you. You must forgive yourself.

FORGIVENESS

*When a relationship collapses,
there needs to come a day when
you can say,
"Will you forgive me for the
things I knowingly and
unknowingly did to be a part of
this relationship failure?"
It may take 20 years to be able
to say it, but it still needs to
be said.*

FORGIVENESS

*Satan is the great
"guilt tripper." He doesn't
want you to be free.
He wants you to live
in the past.*

*The next time Satan wants to
remind you of your past,
remind him of his future!*

*Christ came
that we might have life
and have it abundantly.*

(see John 10:10)

FORGIVENESS

Not forgiving yourself will bring about depression.

In order to grow and to help others, you have to come to terms with forgiving yourself.

There is no condemnation in Christ Jesus.

Rom. 8:1 (NIV)

FORGIVENESS

*The Lord may not have planned
that this should overtake me,
but He has most certainly
permitted it. Therefore, though
it were an attack of an enemy,
by the time it reaches me it has
the Lord's permission and
therefore all is well. He will
make it work together with all
life's experiences for good.*

Paraphrase of Rom. 8:28,
Navigators

FORGIVENESS

*Blessed is he whose
transgression is forgiven,
whose sin is covered.*

Psalm 32:1 (KJV)

*"For I know the plans I have
for you," declares the Lord,
"plans to prosper you and not
harm you, plans to give you
a future and a hope."*

Jer. 29:11 (NIV)

FORGIVENESS

*God looks at you and lovingly
says, "I created you in My
image. I still have plans for you!"*

*...bringing all my energies to
bear on this one thing:
forgetting the past and looking
forward to what lies ahead.*

Phil. 3:13 (TLB)

FORGIVENESS

God does not shoot His own wounded. He forgives and restores.

You are not a "washout"--no matter how you feel!

There are no conditions on God's love, only believe in Him and receive Him.

FORGIVENESS

*God draws you to Himself that
you might know that you are
esteemed and loved.*

*How unlike the nature of God
to ever abandon you.*

YOU matter to God!

FORGIVENESS

Thank Jesus for His forgiveness.

Thank Jesus for the courage He gives you to forgive your offender.

Thank Jesus for the healing He is beginning to do.

FORGIVENESS

*Grace--a freely given,
undeserved, unmerited,
unearnable, and unpayable
favor.*

*And after you have suffered
a little while, the God of all
grace, who has called you to
His eternal glory in Christ will
Himself restore, establish,
and strengthen you.*

I Peter 5:10 (RSV)

FORGIVENESS

Ask God for a tender, honest, transparent heart in dealing with others.

Healing words: "You are going to make it!"

Daily prayer: "Lord, I want to look at others with the eyes of Jesus."

FORGIVENESS

*Restoration is an
ongoing process.*

*Pray that God will use your
healing to encourage and bring
hope to others.*

*When you get on the other side
of healing, you will have an
overwhelming belief that God
loves you.*

FORGIVENESS

*God uses man's evil intentions
to accomplish His purpose.
Joseph said it right when he
told his brothers:
"You intended to harm me.
But, God intended it for good."*

*If only we could see the pattern
of results from God's high
position of insight.*

--Dr. Evan K. Gibson

LOOKING MY BEST

LOOKING MY BEST

*You never have a second chance
to make a good first impression.*

*Be not the first by whom the
new is tried, nor yet last to lay
the old aside!*

*Vanity means "without
purpose--meaningless."
We look good for a purpose!*

LOOKING MY BEST

You are Christ's ambassadors.
You are His representatives.

(See II Cor. 5:20)

The sin is not in looking good,
but in doing less than you can
with a body and personality
that God created in His very
own image.

LOOKING MY BEST

Your beauty should not be <u>dependent</u> on an elaborate coiffure, or the wearing of jewelry or fine clothes, but on the inner personality -- the unfading loveliness of a calm and gentle spirit, a thing very precious in the eyes of God.

I Peter 3:3-4 (Phillips)

LOOKING MY BEST

*Dress for the King! Your image
is always on display.*

*Be fashionable, but modest--a
beautiful combination!*

*If in doubt, it is probably not a
good purchase. Don't buy it!*